DARKNESS FILLS MY HEART

A Book of Poetry

DARKNESS FILLS MY HEART

A Book of Poetry

CASSA PETTY

ISBN: 979-8-9909658-1-2

All rights reserved. No part of this publication may be reproduced, distributed, or transmitted in any form or by any means, including photocopying, recording, or other electronic or mechanical methods, without the prior written permission of the publisher, except for brief quotations embodied in critical reviews and specific other non-commercial uses permitted by copyright law.

Special pricing is available on quantity purchases by corporations, associations, and others. For details, contact the publisher at the email address below.

Orders by U.S. trade bookstores and wholesalers.
Contact: Cassa Petty at cassa.petty@gmail.com

Printed in the United States of America
Publisher: Cassa Petty
Publisher Consultant

SOPHISTICATED PRESS

Dedicated to my mom, my children, Jo Council who pushed me to write this book, and my aunt Paula, who loved books and reading and all things literature.

TABLE OF CONTENTS

Wrote A Book Intro 1
Darkness Fills My Heart 2
My Wings 4
I Built My Own Cage 6
Placed Upon The Shelf! 9
You Drank Of His Words 11
What Is Wrong With You Woman? 14
What Is Wrong With You Man? 16
My Amor's Off 19
You The Fool 22
Give Back My Spine 25
Battle Of Self 29
They Hate My Face 31
Reflection In The Mirror 35
The War Of Self 37
The Longing 40
Release My Shackles 43
A Blessing To You 46
Love Burns Up The Heart 47
Friends We Are Not!! 49
My Queens Crown 51
My Beloved Hair 53
My Mind Is On Fire 56
Only But A Shadow In Time 59
Where To Go 61

I Am A Machine	64
My Heart's Like Stone	67
Fate's Deliverance	70
Goals	71
Let Me Be	72
Acquaintance	73
My Lessons Story	74
My Individual Trip	77
Blindfold Over My Eyes	79
Coccoon Of Growth	80
Who Am I?	81
I Look In Time	82
Deceiver I See	84
Did I Say?	86
Urban Philosophy	88
Hey Black Woman From Chains To Freedom	90
I Tell Myself Lies	93
Your Love Is My Prison	95
She Was A Snake	96
This Is Love	98
The Essence Of Me	99
Beautiful Day	101
She Lived In The Fire	102
Suffocated By His Love	103
Greatness Of You	105
The Pain In My Eyes	106
The End	109

WROTE A BOOK INTRO

Roses are Red
Violets are Blue
I'm not a crook
So I wrote a book
Which of the
Will be of support to me?
Which of the
Will buy a book from me?
Please don't be shook
I know it feels like I have you on the hook.
But please understand I just want you to buy my book.
I spent a lot of time
Writing line by line
Wanting to express
What it is I know best.
I am not a crook
So I wrote this here book.

DARKNESS FILLS MY HEART

Darkness fills my heart so cold
Stoic to danger stoic to foes
Staring at life with no emotion
Walking in place with no devotion
Seeking the warmth of happy bliss
Only to sink further into the dark abyss
Why can't I find true happiness?
It's not a place but a mental state
Still blaming the world for all your woes
Closing the doors to all fortunes told
Hating the people with true success
Claiming the rest can't have what's best
Darkness fills my heart so cold
I can feel my soul no more
As I look on down the street
I care not what fate people meet
I sit out on the corner block
And watch the criminals without shock
As they harass as they taunt
As they shake down the whole block
Stoic to anger stoic to fear stoic to anything in my ear
Stoic to violence
stoic to pain
stoic to the suffering of my fellow man
As I stand in front of this here mirror
I often wonder what has happened here
Whatever happened to this broken life which seems to dislike everyone in sight?
Who hates it here and hates it there and hates it just about everywhere

Lift you head and take sight this is not your only life
You can change and you will too
Open your heart to all that's true
Grow that warmth inside of you
Learn to love with all your might
Learn to love with more than sight
Learn to love with your whole heart
Learn to love from the very start
If you do this with great devotion
You shall have back your emotions.

MY WINGS

And so the time has come
For obstacles to be undone
To stop running with the thrills
To only focus on what's real
Although what it is feels nice
Have to remember there is a price
For I used to sport my wings
And my inner self was clean
Now I don't know what I'm worth
And my lovely wings were taken first
There is confusion in my heart
This makes me wonder where to start
There are illusions in my head
That cause perversions of what is said
I used to know what I am worth
My lovely wings were taken first
When my inner self was clean
I would always sport my pretty wings
I feel bitterness in my heart
You told these lies from the start
What it is you always said
Is what caused illusions in my head
All this neg-a-tivity
Has made my inner self unclean
All this neg-a-tivity
Has made this woman bitter mean
I had forgotten my own worth
So my wings were taken first
I used to fly the heaven skies
Then I became a prisoner to your lies

I look deep inside myself
To search for my inner treasures wealth
A faint spark of fire is left
I just know I can feel the rest
A faint spark of fire is left
As I felt my inner spirits death
I concentrated deeply so
To change that spark into a flow
I feel the bitterness that's left
As it changed to utter emptiness
I feel my inner spark arise
Stroking my inner ego's pride
I can finally feel my worth
But had to feel my soul burn up first
Overcoming my own mind's stings
Gave me back my lovely wings.
Now I know what I am worth
Time to put myself first.

I BUILT MY OWN CAGE

I built up my own cage
I then became filled with rage
I cannot be saved
I perfected my cage
What the hell is wrong with me?
That I don't want to be free
I am so enraged
I built up my own cage
Locked inside my own head
My free will appears to be dead
The decisions I always make
Keep me locked in this place
I don't ever want to know
Where my life just may go
What my future may hold
I just may never know
Some try and break in
To try and save me again
It is not an easy task
In my cage I wear a mask
Once you are let in
You don't know who I am
They look deep into my eyes
Yet I am unrecognized
They leave out of this place
So I can save face
How can they help and save me?
When I don't want to be free?
I am so very much enraged
That I built up my own cage

You can try and break in
But you will never truly win
I have perfected my cage
That is why I am so enraged
I want to be let out
What is this freedom about?
Don't want to be trapped in my own head
Stalled out like the walking dead
Got all lost in my self
Drowning in my inner stealth
My spirit is very unclean
That is why I am so mean
Without some inner silence
We fall out of inner balance
I can feel all the dread
Of being stuck in my head
Let me out of my cell
I am tired of hell
I have become enraged
Preparing my own prison cage
I cannot ever be free
I am too afraid to be me
I give the world a taste
Of my inner gloomy face
They don't like what they see
They don't like what is me
Then I look in the mirror
And the vision gets clear
It is me that hates self
And does not know my own wealth
My consciousness in stealth
So I harm my own health.

I can feel my own rage
So I lock myself in a cage
Now I can see what is truth
Best not to squander my youth
Time to get out of my head
Stop living like the dead
Time to take out the key
Locked up inside of me
Time to open the cell
Of my own personal hell
Time to set my spirit free
So I can be me
Time to let myself out
See what freedom's about

PLACED UPON THE SHELF!

She bottled herself up
And all that other crazy stuff
She was placed upon the shelf
Deterioration of self
So she hated this life
Identified only with strife
She could never see an end
Couldn't even see where to begin
She just knew it all hurt
Trying to live this life curse
She wanted a constant savior
So she could deny her own behaviors
She wanted NO real rights
To her very own life
She wanted to be free
From what she had come to be
She wants to blame you
For what she always knew to be true
She fucked up her own life
To herself blame is just not right
Have to push it off on another
To make herself feel a little better
Have to say it's someone else's fault
Why she bankrupted her inner vault
She bottled herself up
And all that other crazy stuff
She was placed upon the shelf
Detrimental to her own health
She would never really care
If her life would be spared

She just wants to live and grow
Where it black dark and cold
She would never use her wings
She would claim they would cause her life stings
She doesn't want to save herself
She likes to downplay her own wealth
Addicted to her life struggle
She grew to hate her own people
She always loved to play
Self-destructive life games
Refuse to accept her great
She's addicted to her hate
It would be no real surprise
She would like you all to die
She blames all of her life's disasters
On nonrealistic life factors
She bottled herself up
And all that other crazy stuff
She was placed upon the shelf
Until her last disgruntled breath!

YOU DRANK OF HIS WORDS

You loved what you heard
You drank of his words
He promised you the world
Reality and truth were all swirled
You loved what he said
He lived in your head
You loved what you heard
You drank of his words
You thought you knew best
He was better than the rest
You believed what he said
He lived in your head
He said that he cared
Your heart said beware
You loved what you heard
You drank of his words
You heart felt great pain
You felt no love gain
You loved what he said
He lived in your head
He said you were the one
Yet you could tell no one
You tried not to cry
You could not believe it was a lie
You loved what you heard
You drank of his words
You believed what he said
He lived in your head
He would give you small gifts
Yet his heart felt adrift

The calls always came late
You were happy to take the bait
You loved what you heard
You drank of his words
Hotel rooms and your house
Is what it was always about
Never a public date
Or they took place at great lengths
You never heard of this place
Where he took you on a date
Never a place that you know
People may see you come and go
You believed what he said
He lived in your head
You loved what you heard
You drank of his words
It is only you two
Is this love really true
You never meet his friends
All his time he claims they spend
You never met his mother
Yet you're his significant other
You know not his father's name
Yet you can't help but feel ashamed
You loved what you heard
You drank of his words
They appeared to be great
Yet they were only his bait
You believed what he said
He lived in your head
Your heart feels like it will Burst
Your feelings are always hurt

You learn of his wife
Now you wish to take your own life
You knew something was wrong
But you kept going along
You loved what you heard
You drank of his words
You love and you learn
Don't let your heart crash and burn
You are still a beautiful gem
Time to learn to love again
You believed what he said
He lived in your head
Pay attention to the signs
And draw up definite lines
Actions speak louder than words
Leave shallow words for the birds
You loved what you heard
So you drank of his words
Pay attention to how he treats you
That is the heart's reality cue.
If you love what he says
Make sure he acts on what's said.

WHAT IS WRONG WITH YOU WOMAN?

Setting up your whole life around men
Silly woman
Degrading yourself to sell yourself for a cuddle night
Belittled woman
Believing what he says while his actions speak truths
Illusion woman
Putting said man over your children's needs
Delusion woman
Sacrificing self-worth for a love thirst
Idiot woman
Trade in self-respect for a love prospect
Desperate woman
Put nails and weave over necessities
Stupid woman
Stand around and shake ass claiming you come from class
Trifling woman
Teach your daughters the role of common street hoes
Despicable woman
Teach all your sons the common drug runs
Evil woman
Hate your children's dads so you treat your children bad
Spiteful woman
Claiming kids are too lazy yet won't clean up after your own babies
Lazy woman
Getting mad at the kids telling them they won't be shit
Bitter woman
We all know how the story goes God forbid they need clothes
Selfish woman
Their dads want to see the kids yet you say he can't cause you ain't his

Controlling Woman
With their wellbeing you roll the dice God forbid you have to sacrifice
Self-Centered Woman
You have all the latest fashions while the kids have been put on rations
Greedy Woman
A good man comes your way you say you are gonna make him pay
Hateful woman
Claiming you were drunk and totally plastered when you called your children little bastards
Evil Tongue Woman
You count down the days until they are of age
So you can put your children out on their 18th birthday
Ridiculous woman
You claim you did it all by yourself yet discount all your new man's help
Lying woman
You claim the male race is all a disgrace then you plot up against his space
Scorned woman
The babies want to play yet you tell them to go away
Neglectful Woman
Put your bills in the baby's name never to make a payment on the claims
Future ruining Woman
Their dad made their monthly payment you claim he never made it
Devious woman
You contact all his exes and you all plot up how to take his taxes
Conspiring woman
You claim no one will ever love your inner wealth yet you don't even love yourself

BLIND AND CONFUSED ASS WOMAN.

WHAT IS WRONG WITH YOU MAN?

No longer head of the household you put your entire life on hold
No purpose Ass Man
Out here on these streets chasing skirts looking for your next big squirt
Sex Driven Ass Man
Out here helping to make them babies then not taking care of them like you crazy
Family Hating Ass Man
Coming at your woman saying she is your queen then telling her she don't love you if she don't hit the team
Love Destroying Ass Man
Out here claiming that you so famous yet you ain't paid that child support payment
Ole Lying Ass Man
Claiming your love for your children is so deep yet the state had to make that paycheck creep
Delusional Ass Man
Hating on your fellow brother's space claiming you love your entire race
Community Destroying Ass Man
Claiming the other man stole all your gold yet we find you in your brother's billfold
Untrustworthy Ass Man
Sell yourself as a loving and loyal man all the while plotting how to hit your woman's home girl clan
Devious Ass Man
Tell every woman they are the one playing with their hearts just for fun
Evil Ass man

Trade in responsibilities and buy a house now telling your spouse she can hold the house
Future Ruining Ass Man
Claim fatherhood only to your sons and rejecting daughters thinking the world should not be bothered
Female Hating Ass Man
Telling your sons the best way to sex is to go straight in with no protected sex
Crazy Hateful Ass Man
Bragging up on your kids all depends if they can't prove they would enact vengeful revenge
Malice Driven Ass Man
Teaching your children how to hate and telling them there is no such thing as love anyway
Spiteful Ass Man
Talking shit about their mama in their face claiming it's her fault the family is a waste
Shiesty Ass Man
You have yourself the latest Nikes yet your child getting new clothes this year is not very likely
Greedy Ass Man
Explaining to the kids how you had to check in with the warden Cause you stole the latest Jordan's
Thief 'in Ass Man
You became the most despicable of creatures when you started pimping out your sisters
Shady Ass Man
Teaching your children from birth they will never have real worth
Confidence Killing Ass Man
Teaching your son's to become lowlife's by teaching them not to take care of their wife
Family Destroying Ass Man

Telling your son it is only right if he learns to beat his wife
Domestic Violence Ass Man
Telling your daughters she is worth no more than to become some old man's whore
Chauvinistic Ass Man
Convincing yourself of it each day that your mistakes prevent you from living life your way...
Self-Delusion Ass Man
You stopped believing in yourself because you stopped loving in thy self
Self-Hating Ass Man

MY AMOR'S OFF

My armor's off
And now I am lost
My mental shield
Has come to yield
My inner strength
Has felt like weight
The mental games that my mind plays
It brings the pain
I can't feel the gain
I hate this trap
Of my mind's wrath
The pain I feel
It is so real
What am I to learn
From this ordeal
I know the answer
I fight the facts
I cause more suffering
With these very acts
I fight myself
I know what's dealt
My mind's state
At a whims fate
My ego's pride
It burns inside
I feel they bribe me
with fibs and lies
They challenge my spirit
Then think I can't hear it
They insult my intelligence

With their irrelevance
They say take heed
To what they believe
I close my eyes
To look inside
To feel intuition
Of my current situation
I have power inside
That I can't hide
Immune to all
The bitter lies
I trick myself
Say I can't help
Claim I can't see
What is in front of me
Self-discipline is our best friend
Self-belief is our spirit's treat
My will is strong
It is time to move on
Stop self-destruction
That is not my function
Trust my spirit
I know I can hear it
Walk with faith
That is not a waste
The journey is near
Time to conquer your fear
Stop all my self-hate
Time to love what is great
Challenge accepted
I will be self-respected
I will now walk my life

No longer in pain no longer in strife
A new personal love of self all-inclusive with knowledge of self-wealth.

YOU THE FOOL

I see you
Yeah you the fool
Who doubts my strength
And sits around to speculate
How you and yours can take my choice away
You boast and brag
It is all just drag
Now your face scrunched up
Cause you are mad
It is not my fault that you've been had
Deceived by self
Threatened your health
You chose not to recognize women's wealth
Now you want us to act in stealth
You continually try and take our voice
Like it isn't our choice
Barking out threats
Like you the best
You claim you are superior
This proves you more inferior
I sit back and laugh
Due to your acts your brain still lacks
Real intelligence I am not irrelevant
Feel my presence
Acknowledge greatness
I know it's hard
Not to raise your guard
But I don't care
Why you think you scare
You want to bully me

But you a fool to me
These veins pump blood
You aren't the Stud
You can't even tell when you stepped in mud
You try and intimidate
But I laid the bait and could hardly wait
To show you true power
Will be your fate
Open your eyes
Don't tell yourself lies
Look around
Don't be a clown
Know an Alpha don't need no crown
Look in my eyes
Don't even try
You can feel my energy rage up inside
Shed your ego
It is not your hero
Don't get it twisted
I can be quite vicious
So you think my gender
Will stop my splendor and that ultimately I am hindered
I just laugh as I give one last glance
Don't cry now you had your chance
Now I stalk my prey
I'm on my way
I see your weakness
It is your bleakness
I call your bluff
You are not tough
Now you see I can be quite rough
You beg for life

Just like your wife
Yet claim to live a soldier's life
Just bow your head
Your dreams are dead
Illusions shattered in your head
You look up now and now you see
The strength and greatness inside of me

GIVE BACK MY SPINE

Give back my spine
You know it's mine
I learned my place
We were just a waste
I thought you cared
But you were not there
I gave my heart
You tore it apart
I tried to communicate
But it's too late
I've come to see
You are not for me
My soul cries out
What's this all about?
I still want you
God knows that's true
I just had a taste
But it was all a waste
Give back my spine
You know it's mine
I wanted you
But you're not true
You played with my heart
From the very start
I was never blind
When you played with my mind
I just didn't care
Cause I wanted you there
It must have been lust
That's why it's a bust

Gave into temptation
Thinking you were my revelation
But I learned my place
This was all a waste
I chose this life
That caused my strife
I always knew
Your love was not true
But I didn't care
Cause I wanted you there
Give back my spine
You know it's mine
I feel so soft
For what I lost
I don't know why
It was never mine
I knew these facts
Would bring these acts
But I still jumped in
Cause I wanted you then
I still want you now
But I won't bow
I learned my place
And this is all a waste
I cannot want what does not want me
I cannot chase what will not chase me
I will say this
It was not an outright diss
I chose this life
That caused my strife
It was always there
That you did not care

I chose not to see
What was in front of me
I chose this life
Trying to be your wife
When all along
I was the one whom was wrong
You never lied
When I looked in your eyes
It was all right there
That you did not care
I chose to act
Like love was fact
I became obsessed
Like all the rest
My mind is strong
I do not belong
My heart's desire
Has caused mental fire
Give back my spine
You know it's mine
I have now accepted
This is my hearts lesson
I see the signs
You will never be mine
I reclaim my shame
Now I return to fame
I lift my head
Like I always said
Time to clear the clouds from my head
Opened my eyes
I am not blind
Accept myself

I know my wealth
I conquered desire
With my inner fire
I let you go
Cause now I know.

BATTLE OF SELF

I love myself
I hate myself
Fighting off my glorious wealth
Look before you the battle of self
I look inside but what do I see?
I look before me there is just me
I see the good and I see the bad
Oh my god did you see my bad?
I hate myself it is so sad
I was always mad
I was always bad
I never cared who I made so sad
Look over here do you see my good?
It is never ever misunderstood
My love is full it overflows
Never judging where it goes
I love myself
I hate myself
I put myself on a prison shelf
Gave myself to the darker side
Now I feel consequence of pride
The pain is sharp it runs real deep
Never forgotten this pain I keep
Forever witness the battle of self
Look inside to see what's stealth
I look inside what do I see?
It's a better side of me
I give good love
I am real fun
I will always be forever young

I give pure self to all I love
I let them free just like their doves
I love myself
I hate myself
I kill this battle
I am not some cattle
This battle kills me I've had my taste
It is all a waste
of my inner space.

THEY HATE MY FACE

The world is haste
They hate my face
They claim my shine
Like it's not mine
They come from space
And drop their waste
They claim the night
Is not my right
They brag and boast
What they want most
They bring destruction
That is their function
I heard the plots
I heard the plans
I know exactly what
They want with my lands
I know this race
They hate my face
They claim my shine
Like it's not mine
I am a resource
For vacation resorts
They mean it literal
When they say I'm a mineral
They plan to dissect
And take the rest
They plan to leave
quite a bit of mess
They see no value
In our lives

They see no value
To doing right
All they know
Is that I shine
All they see
Is that is mine
I know this race
They hate my face
They claim my shine
Like it's not mine
They plan to gut me
For pure gluttony
They will move here
And spread their fear
They will be corrupt
And run amok
They will seek and destroy
That is their ploy
They will pollute
Down to the root
Now I just need to know
Just what to do
Put on your dark mask
It's not a hard task
Blot out the night
And show no light
Darken the stars
For miles afar
Show them just what
They need to fear
Show them just that
They need you near

When one goes out
In pitch black night
One never knows
How strong his might
What is it out there
That causes strife
What is it out there
Will it take my life
These are the things
That they must see
These are requirements
To leave you be
Leave out a ring of
your shining light
Leave out a ring
To show your might
They will see the light
And remember you
They will see the light
And remember truth
That the night
belongs to you
All the people
Far and wide
Will turn their heads
Up to the sky
Never miss out
On just a glimpse
Of the darkness
Of the eclipse
When you see
the moon again

Always remember
Who is your friend.

REFLECTION IN THE MIRROR

I stand quiet and real still
look at my reflection inside the mirror
I look into my own eyes
there's nothing i see inside
I don't know who is this shell called you
I don't know if what I see is true
my expression is always blank
as I study my own face
my eyes do appear to always be dry
I see nothing is there lurking inside
I feel my presence is very faint
feels like an out of a balance kind of state
I know my head feels very light
I know I feel I have no might
I look into my own eyes
there's nothing i see lurking inside
I try to feel my own heart
can I feel even a little part
I look into the dreaded mirror
It reflects back a deep rooted fear
what if I open up my heart
and it just gets torn all apart
what if i go ahead and give in
how will my life turn out just then
never knew how to surrender
don't know if my soul can take that kind of venture
don't know if it will be worth
what might be a living curse
don't know if a gain can be felt through all the pain
Will this just be another heart stain

I look into my own eyes
I cannot tell myself a lie
I see that there is nothing there
I can see I might not care
I want to learn to love myself
I want to learn how to know my wealth
I want to look into my own eyes
I want to see my soul lurking inside.

THE WAR OF SELF

There's battle here
There's battle there
Mental battles everywhere
The war of self
Where is my wealth
Inner values hidden in stealth
I rush right in
I claim no friends
Never let the love begin
So very afraid
Hide behind the blade
Partaking with others in haterade
Creating a bodily dysfunction
A detrimental self-destruction
Imbalance of the mind body inner junction
A war of self
Can harm your health
A need to restore some inner wealth
I hated the people
Claimed never my equal
I became a very happy sheeple
I was always ashamed
So I shifted the blame
Never took my greatness claim
I became so ignored
I laid down my warrior sword
Nothing in life will be implored
Took a look around
I became emotionally down
I don't want to be this clown

How could this really be
I became all that I see
How can it really be
They are just like me
War of my inner self
Reclaim my inner wealth
Let my inner soul's light
Shine forever star bright
In this life there is growth
So we must know how to let go
You put on many different masks
to conquer many different tasks
You don't become that dreaded mask
It was only use for a certain task
You must always remember this
For Ignorance is hides as bliss
Never become the mask you wear
It is not true it will create inner fears
I am not my life's battles
I am not my life's fight
I don't have to be
forever in the night
Learn to honor what I know
Never shun your new growth
Learn to forgive yourself
For all the lessons life has dealt
Without these obstacles my life would show
I would never advance I would never grow
Without these dreaded life tests
strength wisdom and knowledge would be
Lost at best
I finally see my whole myself

My very essence overflows in wealth
I have so much that I can give
Why should I not really go out and live
Every new day create a new way
Reborn anew
A new chance at you
Give love to yourself
Rebuild your inner wealth
Genuine self-love in your entirety
Without totality growth is not very likely
If you want to know what it takes to grow
You have to be willing to go
Where your scared to go
Total love of oneself
Total acceptance of oneself
brings forth recognition
Of depressions mental prisons
A balance of your essence
Restores your superior presence

THE LONGING

My soul longs for you
So pure and true
I feel so blue I am not with you
No longer whole
You stole my soul
Oh yes it's true I do want you
I'd trade in all my ways
If you would stay
Heart cries out through space
I want to kiss your face
Can you feel my essence
All around your presence
The pain my heart bears
It so wants to be there
No longer whole
You stole my soul
This pain runs deep
This love I keep
Can't trade it in
Where would I begin
Consumed by you
My love is true
I'm not with you
That's why I'm blue
We are so far apart
It breaks my heart
My heart's inflamed
It screams your name
With my strongest desires
You light my love's fire

My heart doesn't care
Although it is scared
To be true to you
Don't you hurt me boo
My heart has been run through
It wants something new
I can no longer ration
My inner love's passion
Here in my own place
I had to leave this space
My soul floats out
There is no doubt
Of where it goes
It wants your soul
No longer whole
You stole my soul
No more heart control
My love is bold
It has come prepared
To drop being scared
To allow love in
Penetrate through my skin
Like a cloud of smoke
My soul you invoke
My soul reaches out
No more love drought
You are all In my chest
My heart just can't rest
My mind is consumed
By the essence of you
My mind gets confused
My heart does not want to bruised

I will not take the bait
Run from love's great fate
Where ever it is you go
My heart's desire will flow
Like smoke through the air
You soul calling me near
I can't help this heart's state
You are forever my mate
My love takes no blame
For who it inflames
I have no silly shame
For my heart's love flame
I will commit to flow
Where my heart goes

RELEASE MY SHACKLES

I know it's me
That is not really free
My mental chains
Cause me mental pains
I free myself
To retrieve mental health
Free like the dove
I free my self-love
I set ME free
So I can BE
I release my mind
To love what's mine
I see this mental cell
I created my mental hell
I release this accepted curse
To reverse once accepted worst
I open my eyes
I step outside
All the external lies
I will not hide
I am a real ride and die
I feel the weight
has left my space
I will not continue to worry
About what's blurry
I have already acknowledged
I had a mental blockage
I must conquer all of self
To reverse self-hate I have dealt
It is not an easy task

To remove the external mask
But I will commit
To what I will benefit
I have cleaned my chakra channels
Now released my mental shackles!

Suffocated by his love
She guarded him like none above
You meant to play him in mental games
She meant to put you into a shallow grave
You meant to hurt his very heart
She meant to tear you all apart
You meant to knock him to his knees
She meant to cut down your family trees
Suffocated by his love
She guarded him like none above
Her love for him was always true
And her love for him always grew
Her love for him was very deep
Perhaps a little bit too steep
She watched his every waking move
Her heart was very much confused
She felt he could never love or want her
So she would be his silent protector
She stood off in the distance
And prepared for her protector's vengeance
She craved his love and warm embrace
It was his rejection she could not take
She would love him from a distance
But you will feel wrath from her penance
If you hurt him watch your back
It will be your head that she will crack

You will surely be alone
When she breaks your skull and bones
It will be you your living essence
when it comes up missing will make no difference
It will be your life your very soul
That will prove to be no more.
Suffocated by his love
She wanted nothing more above.

A BLESSING TO YOU

May you forever go far
With everything that you are
May there be no inner hate
As your essence is forever great
May you never grow tired
Building yourself up from the fire
It is never too late
To build and to create
Whatever it is you need
Resides inside your inner being
It was always only up to you
If you will build your life in doom
It will always be your choice
If you will stand behind your voice
If you will stand firm
When your life takes that turn
Will life be your way
Can you rule your own day
Do you know your own power
How it can make you or devour?
May you find your life's place
And may you own your own life's space
May you find your inner peace
May your mental turmoil be deceased
May you love the self you see
May that self forever be

LOVE BURNS UP THE HEART

Love burns up the heart
It will surely tear it all apart
The love pains have begun
Oh shit you are the one
What is this shit I feel?
Can I make an immediate appeal?
This love shit really hurts
Can't we deal with this shit first?
There seems like there's no end
The love pains flare up again
Love burns up the heart
It will surely tear it all apart
I swear it feels like death
With every passing of my breath
Please never leave my side
Your love is my trusted guide
This love shit really hurts
Can't we deal with this shit first?
My heart belongs to you
This much I know is true
I love your very essence
I thank the heavens when I'm in your presence
I wake up thinking of you
I go to sleep dreaming of you too
My mind fills up with passion
You are my only distraction
I want to be with you
This much I know is true
Love burns up the heart
It will surely tear it all apart

Love flames cause great pain
As your love burns me again
I can't help but to stay blue
Cause I'm not there loving you
I want to touch upon your face
I want to feel your warm embrace
I want blend with your soul
As our love will make us whole
I want to be the strongest backbone
You will never again be left alone
This passion is my only distraction
Yet it brings me great satisfaction
I am learning to deal with the yearning
I am dealing with the love of mine you are stealing
This love shit really hurts
Can we deal with this shit first?
There are no guarantees
There will always be a you and me
Yet I will not tell a lie
And say I don't want to try
You are a part of me
I will never escape from thee
Your love has got me scared yet I do not seem to care
I want to know the you
That wants to know me too
This love shit really hurts
Can we deal with this shit first?

FRIENDS WE ARE NOT!!

If I had to choose
I would never allow myself to be used.

Never be misled
by those I thought to be my friend.

Never gave my heart
so they could break it all apart

Never shared my essence
so they could feel my inner presence...

I would never waste my breath talking to you like you were more than just a guest

I would never give you all my trust
So you can use my trust to bring me to dust.

I would never believe in you
Because for you it's only about what I can do for you

If I had to choose I would never feel abused

I would accept the behavior queues and know you were never true

I would never feel disgraced
as I look upon your face

I would never feel it was a waste
to share my time and my personal space

I'm tired of all you fakes
Thinking you can manipulate what was always great.

Taking my generosity
As if we are in some democracy

I don't owe you shit
what I do is for my own personal bliss

But it does make me pissed
when you think I'm here to diss.

Thinking you can use me up
Like I'm too dumb to see what's up

Like I'm here to be at your beck and call
Yet I can't depend on none of y'all

Banking on we old school homies
as the only reason you feel you know me.

Get the fuck outta here with that shit!

I'm not some naive and stupid bitch!

MY QUEENS CROWN

It is not some dream
that I am a queen
I have no traditional crown
but I'm not feeling down
My crown is real
No one can steal
It's bound to my head
Yes that's what I said
I have a crown
but not made of gold
I honor my crown
with no stones in mold
No precious gems
No material items
Just a royal crown
Never taken down
My crown is real
No one can steal
Let down my mane
There is no shame
My crown is there
Displayed as hair
Underneath it all
My royalty calls
I am a queen
That is no dream
Don't need your approval
For myself I rule over
I live for me
I know what I see

I control all the confusion
In my inner world's illusions
I pass all the laws
For my inner self's cause
I enforce all my will
That is my inner pact deal
I hold this crown
Never taken down
You can't steal shit
Never to benefit
You want to know
Where my crown goes
You don't ever believe
What you can't see
You want to take
What belongs to me
I AM this crown
Don't care if you frown
Just like I said
For this you may dread
Where is my crown?
The crown's MY HEAD!

MY BELOVED HAIR

They really hate my hair
But I do not care
They all can't help but stare
They really hate my hair
They offer me up wigs
Said try this ya dig
I look in their face
What a sad disgrace
They really hate my hair
I do not even care
They reach out to touch my hair
Big eyed with blank stares
They suggest yet again
What extensions to put in
They say it looks nappy
Like that equates to crappy
They say to look professional
I must go all unnatural
They really hate my hair
Yet I just cannot care
I love my own mane
Yours is not the same
So don't be so lame
Tell me to be the same
I love my own hair
I just do not care
If you want to stare
It brings out my flare
I will not change me
I know what I see

A beautiful queen
Her hair is so clean
I know just what I mean
There is no need to demean
Just like the beloved tree roots
Strength branches out from my hair's shoots
I love my own mane
Funny how they call me so strange
I love how I was birthed
I'm a part of this earth
There is no mistakes
In god's way to create
You can keep your hair perm
Self love is the best thing to learn
They really hate my hair
I just cannot care
All they do is stare
At my amazing hair
I can feel their envy
Just like an enemy
They lay out the straight tracks
And the natural hair attacks
Tell me to try and fit in
I need to look just like them
They bring out the little box
Yet claim there are no mental locks
Just put the weave in
Smile and say "see you fit in"
Don't you just love yourself
With this new outer wealth
The clone in the mirror
Fills me up with great fear

That reflection is not me
How can I love the reflection of thee?
The reflection is a fake
Who walks around with a stake
Stabbing at her own heart
Tearing her confidence and self-love apart
They really hate my hair
Yet I just cannot care
It will always be a part of me
And we are what we be
I will not alter my hair
So that you will not stare
I will not alter my hair
So that you will not fear
Be comfortable with yourself
No one but you brings your wealth
Be in love with yourself
Build up lasting health
Your hair is your crown
Let no one tear it down
Always love who you are
Continue to be a shining star
Take care of your hair
Give them something worth the stare!

MY MIND IS ON FIRE

My mind is on fire
My heart is a liar
You tell me it's true
Then why am I always blue
My heart is at stake
Yet you bring it heartache
My mind is on fire
My heart is a liar
If my actions were dealt
The way that it is that I felt
I would not even turn
As I watched the world burn
If my mouth would only speak
All the deceptions I have had to defeat
My tongue would only stun
And send your ego on the run
I go back and undo
What you said to me was true
You bring me disgrace
When I look upon your face
You insult my very essence
When I see your very presence
My mind is on fire
My heart is a liar
I believed in you
And you were never true
I hate myself for the day
I let you in my heart to stay
You look at me as dumb
My actions were just numb

I chose the path not to react
to the person holding me back
I disrespected self
Now I want to take your health
I need to calm my nerves
My ego has been heard
My mind is on fire
My heart is just a liar
Now I know the truth of heart
It s to tear you all apart
I want to far grow above
This obstacle called love
I don't want to feel this shit
I am having mental fits
When I look into the mirror
My eyes are filled with fear
Can I build a wall around it
act like it never really happened
can I just forget this shit
and forget you do exist
I hate this feeling in my heart
Its tearing my chest all apart
My mind is on fire
My heart is just a liar
I think I know what is really best
Just that time to take a spiritual rest
I need to back up from this scene
I need to assess just what it means
There is a lesson I must learn
So I can stop having to feel the burn
I will figure out what it is
So I never feel this again

ONLY BUT A SHADOW IN TIME

Only but a shadow in time
My soul cries out then it whines
I never did go out in the world and live
I never did help out in the world and give
I never really did what I knew I should
Although I said that I always would
Never sought out betterment of self
Only stole each other's wealth
Only but a shadow in time
My soul cries out and then it whines
I never sought out this thing called love
I never really thought that it really was
If someone's love could be that true
Someone to love you through and through
Who could look upon your ugly face
And still claim they love you anyway
Who can see you at your very worst
And still want their love to be your first
Only but a shadow in time
My soul cries out and then it whines
I never did fall in love when I could have
I never gave love to my family when I should have
I never did give all of myself
To build up my inner life's wealth
My heart is so cold it lacks compassion
My heart is so cold it knows not some passion
If I could be given one more chance
I would give all my love in advance
I would let my inner guards come crashing down
I would not waste any time playing around

I would give out my whole entire heart
I would do this act from the very start
I would cry out when I was in pain
I would not run from my heart's inner stains
Only but a shadow in time
My soul cries out and then it whines
I cheated myself of inner wealth
I did not love I stole from self
I walked this path all alone
I walked this path with a heart of stone
If I had the opportunity to try again
My love would radiate out through my skin
If I detect pain within your face
My love would take you from this place
I really want to know about this thing they call love
I want to learn to fit with someone like a glove
I know that I want to learn to really care
I'm tired of always having this love scare
I look inside my body my heart's gears have died
what I would give today to have love's last try
Only but a shadow in this time
Can I experience real love even just one time?

WHERE TO GO

You step in fright
Try and test my might
You best to brought your friends
My wrath is now to begin
My eyes like ice
I will NOT be nice
Battle is my vice
I will take your life
I think you should know
It's just best you go
Don't fuck with me
I can be quite mean
If you must insist
I will bring my fist
You force regulation
You teach separation
You claim you will help
While you squander wealth
You force and you oppress
Yet claim you know what is best
Just look outside
You know you cannot hide
You see the result
Yet you claim no fault
Was it not your choice
To remove our voice
I dig deep inside
Pull from the fire inside
My rage from within
Radiates through my skin

I open my mouth
So the truth can come out
The heat from inside
Burns out through my eyes
I must advocate
Help save the human race
It's like an alien chase
Trying to get to space
I hope you all know
This is not our home
We have burnt it on up
Running all amok
I have a deep devotion
To help change the commotion
To build up again
What we had back then
We have too many hungry forces
With our current resources
Running out of livable space
To balance the human race
The children are starving
Their mothers are crying
All the while their fathers are dying
Don't trust the media it is always lying
Pumping their head
With everything dead
Taking their worth
Reprogramming with dirt
Unleash the undead
Claiming they are quality led
Steal from the earth
Everything she has birthed

Open your eyes
Everything is a lie
We must get off this earth
So we can have a rebirth
As it currently stands
Earth needs not of man
Look a little closer
We're like a virus in nature
Drained our precious earth
For all she is worth
We weren't even nice
When we stripped her life
Nothing's left
We tried our best
Time to go
We all should know
But you say we must be led
Get out of our heads
We will never be led
But we do not know
Just where is it we want to go.
Now you see how the story goes
Time to feel overpopulation woes.

I AM A MACHINE

I am a machine
That's why I am so mean
I am a machine
So I follow routines
I'm locked in my head
So my spirit is dead
I am a machine
No freedom is deemed
My mental cap screams
I want to believe
In the life that I see
I am a machine
My structure is unclean
I have no foundation
I follow regulation
I am a machine
My will is unseen
My battery runs low
As my ego takes a blow
My battery runs low
With every repeated blow
I will not think for myself
I have no mental wealth
I will not think for myself
Personal agenda in stealth
I am a machine
My face is unseen
Uncomfortable with self
I have sabotaged my own health
Uncomfortable with self

Sacrificed my self's wealth
I am a machine
Personal freedom is unseen
I am a machine
Personal freedom not deemed
To pass this life test
I must be like the rest
That is the illusion
That we have all gladly chosen
A total loss of myself
Took a toll on my health
A total loss of myself
Great anger will be dealt
I am a machine
My choices unseen
I am a machine
Responsibility should be king
Detach from the collective
I gain new perspective
Detach from the collective
I remove myself from the wreckage
I was a machine
Now my soul is quite clean
I was a machine
But now I have found me
I will be who I be
I will see what I see
I will do whatever I can pull from inside of me
I can think for myself
I have inner wealth
I don't need your attention
I have a life goal mission

I can stand by myself
I don't need no help
I don't have to be mean
For I am my own queen
I was a machine
I looked through a fake screen
I was a machine
Bad habits are cleaned
I lift up my head
Compulsions are dead
I lift up my head
I put self-delusion to bed
I will make a way
I mold my own clay
I have killed my machine
My mind is back with me
I have killed my machine
Time I live out what I need.

MY HEART'S LIKE STONE

My heart's like stone
I walk alone
They are all some clones
So I walk alone
My path is bleak
I have known defeat
They all say they care
With dead blank stares
Look into their soul
I can see the mole
Little do they know
I will walk alone
I don't need the fake
For it brings out hate
I don't need untrue
I prefer virtue
My heart's like stone
I hate these clones
They test my faith
Sometimes they bring disgrace
They bring out my emotion
It's like my inner rage potion
I just hate the fake
It is all over the place
I have to complete my mission
There will be no division
Get out of my vision
I have a self-growth mission
I don't need you
With that I withdrew

I always knew
A clone is untrue
My heart's like stone
I hate these clones
Pretend they care
With dead blank stares
Sabotage my way
Brings their last day
Conquer my inner demons
My soul's eye awakens
I walk alone
Cause I am no clone
I'll find my way
I will never stay
I just hate this place
So I must vacate
My heart like stone
Always to walk alone
My heart's like stone
I will be alone
I do not want you
You are never true
I do not want you
Who thinks I have no clue
I walk through the gate
With strong mental state
I defeat the hate
I am that great
My Journey's long
I will be so strong
You do not belong
In my story's song

Stand aside
I have great pride
Stand aside
While I conquer my life
Don't be surprised
I will tell no lies
I will do this alone
For I am no clone

FATE'S DELIVERANCE

With my head looking down
you thought I was oblivious to what lurks around
You planned and plotted against my being
It's my wrath you will be seeing
You tricked yourself with your own lies
When you thought my beast did not have eyes
I saw your shiesty-ness at its best
You damn fool I'm not like the rest
You thought I'd run from battles or from war
You have no clue I beg for more
I know the battlefield is my home
My life's path was surely shown
The real question you should ask
Is why fate delivered me your ass
For if your crooked self slithered into my presence
You must be due for them hard life lessons
I do not fear I know what's near
I'm not scared War I can bare
With your back against the wall
You should have taken heed to my warrior call

GOALS

I lift up my head and I look ahead
My path is long I must be strong
I am not scared for I've come prepared
I am not weak for I have belief
I know my plan it has begun
My journey's long but I belong
Can you feel my presence?
Do you know my confidence?
Does it even matter in my journey's ladder?
No time for talk I'm on my walk
Can't stop to play I'm on my way.
Can't be put on hold it's time
to achieve my goals.

LET ME BE

No playing
No games
No lies and no wastes of time
I'm here no fear
There are no tears
I feel no stings
I have big wings
I just don't care
You had your share
I know you see
just let me be...

ACQUAINTANCE

Most of you SEE me but you cannot see into my soul
No matter what you hear or whatever you were told

Yes you do see me yes in the flesh.
You look upon my face and think you know my place

Harsh reality is always best so I put your illusion to the test
Although you do see me you will never really KNOW me

What you see is your illusion and is not a part of me
That person that you think I am is not a face of me

That mask that you see and think I have become to be
Is the puppet pulled by strings that society's box has created me to be.

The fact you cannot see
when you claim you want to know me
Is that fact I saw the best
When I put your inquiries to the test
You wondered who is she?
You say you want to know me
Yet you never took the time
To really glance into my shine.

MY LESSONS STORY

I am sometimes slow to learn
But in the end I always see.
There is a seed of enlightenment
Brewing up inside of me
I have overcome the ugly trenches
Of my unhealthy worldly wishes
I will not stand aside
Why you think I ran to hide
I am not scared of what comes next
There isn't an issue I can't best
Sometimes we trick ourselves with lies
And say we cannot control our lives
That it is not my fault at all
That my character took its fall
Then we blame all those around us
For the conditions we were in when they found us
Then we tell them it's their fault
Our life's prosperity came to halt
But not me I know the truth
Only I control my youth
Only I control my mind
Only I control the lies
That I choose to accept
What I knew was never best
I created my own fate
When I gave into my hate
It was always my own fault
When I broke my inner vault
When I gave into temptation
And set up my own damnation

We look with eyes full of lust
Yet blame our loved ones for their trust
Giving into worldly passions
Blaming others for our own actions
Not with me not today
I want to live my life my way
I'll take responsibility for my own actions
Try not to give in to distractions
There is a reason for my choice
Maybe I should not cry yet rejoice
I have to learn from my mistakes
That what I do may come back as fate
Those are my lessons to have learned
I must not act like I am not concerned
If I don't learn from this lesson
It will come back in replication
I must accept this as my fact
And make myself a growth pact
That what I decide to do today
Is for the betterment of my own way
You may think what you experience is cold
Yet in reality it is your life journey's gold
You should always want to forgive
What it is you yourself have lived
These lessons are critical to self
And they build up your self's wealth
Never shun what you have done
Know life is not always fun
Never hate what you create
And sit around and speculate
Learn to love your life's lessons
And learn to appreciate the message.

MY INDIVIDUAL TRIP

I'm on my way out headed on a long trip
once at my destination i won't need shit
I will not tell a lie this is a one way trip
With no ETA for a return home ship

If for some reason I indeed do return
You will wonder what happened to make me so stern
You will sense all my power you will sense all my strength you will sense all the time I will not let you waste

For on this long journey before she came back
She found out what moved her and what held back
She found out her friends she found out her foes
she found out who hated her behind closed doors
She found out what makes her and that nothing can break her

She found out there is nothing to fear but her maker
She learned who she is she already knew who she was She knew life's journey was not all fun
She grabbed her life's reins and march with her fist
She handled everything that came out of the mist
She found a great treasure one you can't win
She finally became comfortable in her own skin

She loves who she is and loves who she was
She loves all life's burdens and holds no grudge
I need that experience i need that pain
so I can grow stronger and move without strain.
I need that hardship I need sometimes to fret
So i can understand i can beat all this shit

There is nothing in this world i can't do
There is nothing in this world like you.

BLINDFOLD OVER MY EYES

I tie this blindfold across my eyes
I listen quietly with no surprise
For what it is I usually see
is nothing more but fakery
I close my eyes I listen still
All my senses come to hilt
What it is I hear I feel
Focused on it feels so real
What I feel and what I sense
Is your rebuttal to my happiness
I close my eyes I hear your cries
But I'm no longer affected by your lies
I've heard your cries
I tried I tried but I all got was more of your lies
I tie this blindfold across my eyes
I tie this blindfold I say goodbye.

COCCOON OF GROWTH

I ball my fist you know I'm pissed
I speculate as I stew in hate
I grasp the facts of my minds trap
What's not the truth what is illusion
As I contemplate your intrusion
How dare you mess with me I'm GREAT how dare you mess with your own fate
I wonder how I am so cold I wonder how I became so bold
I've dreamt of paradise I want true bliss
How can I have it what's happiness?
I hide myself in this cocoon I hide myself and ponder gloom
I speculate what I have faced I speculate how I conquered dire straits
I've fought many battles I've faced many wars
I know things can change I know there's more
I hide myself in this cocoon I feel refreshed I feel brand new
I feel a break and now I'm straight I am afoot on god's green earth
I feel the love I feel we're one
New understanding new trains of thought
New possibilities new life's crop
New opportunities I'll be on top
Mind's eye awakening eyes open up
I feel the energy I feel the strength
I fear no enemies I have walked great lengths
I lift my head I walk along
I chose my path and my will is strong.

WHO AM I?

Who am I
That's why I cry
Who am I
I think I died
Who are you
Oh I'm true
Well who are you?
I'm you too
What did you say?
Am I in a daze?
Who are you
If I'm you too?
Who am I?
Don't tell a lie?
Who am I
That's why I cry
For who i am
Is what i was
Who I am
Is just because
Well if I am you and you are I
Then why just is it we both cry
Well that is easy
I'll tell you a taste
Just where is it
We call our face?
Just where is it
It left this place.

I LOOK IN TIME

I look in time
Guess what I find
I am so blind
How could this be?
I cannot see
The path laid out in front of me
For what is gold
Should be your goals
And I have none
My paths undone
I sit and wait
For some sort of fate
This is the biggest
Of my mistakes
This causes you
To procrastinate
There is a mission
There is a goal
Look inside for what is foretold
It is your duty and yours alone
To build your life and not be a clone
You are the creator
Of your own fate
Don't you want to live something great?
Plan out your future
Don't even wait
Better do this with great haste
Plot out your mission
With great intension
Then watch your life

Take on new dimension
Next thing you know
Like it hit you with a blow
You will look in time
And you will see just fine.

DECEIVER I SEE

OH so now you're all for me
Well that is not what I see
Compliments should be a lot
But should we say compliments are NOT
Well at least not for me
But let me tell you what I see
You can show concern and love to other women
Try and show them you are better than their own men
While leaving your own significant other
To fend for her her kids you and every other
Spending time looking to council every other woman
While leaving your own lady to self-council her own depression
Always promising her the great life
While you inbox any other man's wife
Never showing any financial motivation
Unless there is a self-benefitting foundation
Will you help you own woman with the bills? hell no
But will help Joe Blow's girl with her house note
Financial drains are all the same
Once used up they run amok
Try and convince you that you cause them depression
When all you ever been to them was a blessing
Being the true head of the house
While acting smaller than a mouse
Another method to pacify your self-denial
All the while trying not to focus on your betrayal
Maybe you are not in denial at all
Maybe it is I who has taken that fall
The signs were all here I had all the clues
That you were not a man who could be true

Energy doesn't lie
That's why it feels tense when you hide
Pretending you can't stand the ringer tone
Yet turn it back on when you are alone
Taking your phone into the bathroom
Is the only time your phone gets any action
Hour and a half bathroom session
Now you won't look at me or even hold conversation
Now we are sleeping on opposite sides of the bed
While I figure out what the fuck is going on in my head
Everything is right here front stage and center
I don't have to sink by the hand of my love's counterfeiter
I can accept the facts of what I see
And learn what it's me that accepts what's beneath me
I can acknowledge that fact and make myself a pact
To focus on self and focus on health

DID I SAY?

It's a new day
so i have to say
You are so fly
I wanna cry
I love your lips
Can I have a kiss
You are so fine
Your body's divine
All I want to do
Is make love to you
Protect your heart
From poison darts
Kiss your lips
And thrust my hips
Fill you rise
From my insides
You know it's true
I love what you do
I cannot hide
The joy inside
When I see you
I wanna be with you
Give me your heart
And all other parts
With you by my side
I cannot hide
My heart's desire
To be love's fire
And fill you up
With love and stuff

My heart is stacked
To have your back
With you by my side
I cannot hide
God's favor for me
He gave me a king
I am so blessed
He gave me the best.

URBAN PHILOSOPHY

I'm gonna hold it down
I don't mess around
I will never drown
I know how to get down
I'm not with this shit
but we will handle it
our time is near
just look at their fear
their most scared of us
they are just so jealous
We have a plan
it has began
put on your boots
and gain some solid roots
our journey right now is hard
but our goals are not far
do not despair
we will repair
the time we lost
we were never bossed
you knew I would miss you
and feel like I'm lost
put on your armor
it won't be much longer
The battle's begin
at a moments whim
we are prepared already
the struggles are quite heavy
just look into my eyes
it should be no surprise

I am not scared
we have come quite prepared
we are not afraid
for it was we who set the stage
our time is close
what I want the most
our struggles will end
and our new life will begin.

HEY BLACK WOMAN FROM CHAINS TO FREEDOM

What is your worth?
Did you know it from birth?
That you are a queen
Never to be demeaned!
You deserve the best
Never give your dreams a rest
You can have it all
Just remember to stand tall
Never let your standards fall
Thinking you cannot have it all
That is just a lie
Don't let that slip on by
What others think of you
Is not your business boo
So don't worry about the perceptions
Or fitting into others definitions
You are beautiful through and through
No need to create another you
Stand by your own integrity
To feel your soul's prosperity
Never stand so mean
that your inner soul can't be clean
I will not let you label me
I will never be who you see
I am entitled to my inner battles
This does NOT reduce me to your shackles
I understand my entire self
I have total acceptance of my own wealth
I don't need an external factor
To build me up by benefactor

I know all I need to be
Is already resonating inside of me.
I love who I have become
And I don't need external love
I feel my heart inside my chest
Is more beautiful than all the rest
I know I am full of wonderful strength
I'm so strong and my strength goes great lengths
My beautiful lioness heart
Does stand so far apart
From the ugliness you see
And claim is a part of me
No need to hide myself inside
My heart's full of raging pride
I know I deserve true love
That floats so high above
I know I deserve much respect
No not a false love prospect
Return to me what I return to you
And everything with us will always stay true
Never downgrade yourself to pick up unvalued wealth
Never hide your true self
It hazardous to your own health.
Always know you are worth
Everything that you birthed!
Whether good or bad
we are all we had
Never knock yourself
For mistakes made by self
Never hate your strife
It builds up strong life
Always love self to the very end

You will always be your only real friend!

We are all our own creators of self-love self hate happiness or disasters!

Birth GREATNESS into your life. Never settle for what is beneath you. And never hide yourself behind the labels of sheep who will never really KNOW you as they are looking for distractions from their own self-mastery and life journey lessons and will try and label YOU as their self-build up tool.
They pull all said self-hate and self-doubt and deflect it on to you so they can look their own selves in the face and not feel disgraced!! ***

I TELL MYSELF LIES

My guardian angel always cries
I intentionally blind my own eyes
To my very own surprise
I found I tell myself the best of lies
It was I who imprisoned me
In my own personal penitentiary
It is I whose mind runs all amok
It is I who locks myself up
I ignore what is known as fact
To create my own victim acts
Hating eyes always at my back
Always ready for that imminent attack
The outgrowing of my human shell
Worries the simpletons of coming hell
They talk much in a state of hate
And yet I always take the bait
I end up with a horrible fate
The destined fate that I create
Found myself to be scared of love
Always scared to rise above
Scared of my own success
Scared to be my very best
Stopped making my own decisions
Started asking for external permissions
I had dropped my inner fire
To become a successful liar
Just look into my eyes
My soul already died
Can you see all my grief
My total loss of self-belief

My attitude has grown so cold
I have lost my inner gold
I must shed my toughest skin
I must look deeper within
I must quit with all the hate
Must learn to love to self-regulate
Pull the wool from my own eyes
Got to stop with all the lies
Feel that my self-transformation
Is in full anticipation
I cannot really go and hide
From the greatness that's inside
Tired of all my biased lies
That killed my inner pride
Tired of all my self-induced hate
You know that hate that I create
Tired of all life's stings
I spread my wings
I cut my mental chains
Only I remain
Without all the hate
Now I can self-create
Without all the mental strife
I can build a new life
Now time to start again
A new life to begin
No more self-limiting sin
Now it's time to win!

YOUR LOVE IS MY PRISON

Your love is my bondage
I am forever your loving hostage
Your love is so very deep
It woke my heart from its slumber sleep
It will always be fact and it's true
My love belongs to you
My heart is no longer stone
I am no longer left alone
Your kisses touch my soul
You will always make me whole
When you hold me I must confess
I know that love knows what is best
You accept me for who I am
You are worth more than any gem
No matter what it is I claim
There is nothing better than your love chains
They say that love will send you crashing
But those who say that know not love or passion
You are the other side of me
With you I can finally BE
You are my lover you are my best friend
Our love is pure it will never end!
I put my wrists out I'm not so tough
I wish to be incarcerated in your love's cuffs!
Take me away go lock me up
Nothing can corrupt us I'm love struck!
I volunteer to be in my heart's prison
Your love brings me total freedom!

SHE WAS A SNAKE

She was a snake
with a gorgeous face
and with all that she touched
It would slice at your guts
Her words were venomous poison
As you felt your soul's erosion
With her poisonous kiss
You felt your heart being dissed
You would not believe the truth
She would never be good to you
A snake is always a snake
You are on her dinner plate
Guard your heart well
You better bid her farewell
If you stay around
You can only be knocked down
She never hisses she only bites
She will destroy your heart's delight
A snake is always a snake
Don't find yourself on her dinner plate!

A quick poem for my brothers!

Snakes come in all forms man or woman!

Respect what you are dealing with. They all show their true face at some time the real trick is to accept what it is you see!

Sisses this poem can be in reverse also but the image was female hence....poem for the bruh's!

THIS IS LOVE

This is love so he had been told
Yet when he looked up she had sucked out his soul
He thought she was best
But she stole all of his breath
He thought she would care
She sucked out all his air
He was blinded by beauty
Her love was off duty...

THE ESSENCE OF ME

The essence of me
Is stronger than thee
The power of me inside
Resonates strong on my outside
They look in my eyes
They are intimated inside
They can feel power in my energy
Their soul's drops to down to spirit knees
Why do you always fear
Whenever I am so near
I can tell you why
My words are not a lie
You earned the face of a coward
So your soul have become soured
Your life has no desires
So you start internal fires
You look at what I do
And feel your life is through
Why ever you look at what others do
And feel you don't have the power to make moves too
That fact Is sad within itself
You know not your own wealth
So you hate upon me
Cause I grow my own seeds
I plant my own desires
I build my own empire
I walk my own path
Don't get caught up in my wrath
Your soul has become so shallow
Your life has become empty and hollow

I am a warrior by nature
I send all haters to their maker
You stalk out my inner grace
And try to mimic my external face
There is power inside of you
You need to believe that shit is true
I can never be replaced
Nor can I ever be erased
If you know what's best for you
You should take heed to my message queue
And get out of my space
Or your life will be a waste!

BEAUTIFUL DAY

Have a beautiful day
In every possible way
Why not let your mane down
There is no need to frown
While your hair flows on down
Your hair is your crown
So let it hang down
Always love your natural crown
Now on to the day
We can have it our way
How do we do that you say
Why not plan out your day
And you can have it your way
Just need to make up your mind
That the day will be divine
This is your universe
Will it be a blessing or a curse
The choice is up to you
No need to start off being blue
Today will be a good day
Now remember to keep it that way!

SHE LIVED IN THE FIRE

She was in love with the dragon

Her heart full of passion

She would dance with fire

You could never feel higher

She lived her life in the fire

To soothe her inner heart's desire.

SUFFOCATED BY HIS LOVE

Suffocated by his love
She guarded him like none above
You meant to play him in mental games
She meant to put you into a shallow grave
You meant to hurt his very heart
She meant to tear you all apart
You meant to knock him to his knees
She meant to cut down your family trees
Suffocated by his love
She guarded him like none above
Her love for him was always true
And her love for him always grew
Her love for him was very deep
Perhaps a little bit too steep
She watched his every waking move
Her heart was very much confused
She felt he could never love or want her
So she would be his silent protector
She stood off in the distance
And prepared for her protector's vengeance
She craved his love and warm embrace
It was his rejection she could not take
She would love him from a distance
But you will feel wrath from her penance
If you hurt him watch your back
It will be your head that she will crack
You will surely be alone
When she breaks your skull and bones
It will be you your living essence
when it comes up missing will make no difference

It will be your life your very soul
That will prove to be no more.
Suffocated by his love
She wanted nothing more above.

GREATNESS OF YOU

May you forever go far
With everything that you are
May there be no inner hate
As your essence is forever great
May you never grow tired
Building yourself up from the fire
It is never too late
To build and to create
Whatever it is you need
Resides inside your inner being
It was always only up to you
If you will build your life in doom
It will always be your choice
If you will stand behind your voice
If you will stand firm
When your life takes that turn
Will life be your way
Can you rule your own day
Do you know your own power
How it can make you or devour?
May you find your life's place
And may you own your own life's space
May you find your inner peace
May your mental turmoil be deceased
May you love the self you see
May that self forever be

THE PAIN IN MY EYES

The pain in my eyes
I cannot lie
You cannot deal
With how I feel
My struggles and strife
Would take your life
You cannot deal
With how I heal
The pain in my eyes
I cannot lie
I want to kick
And tear up this shit
I want to pound
All of you to the ground
I want to destroy everything in the town.
The pain in my eyes
I cannot lie
I cannot hide
The pain inside
I lift my fist
Then you all shit
Cause you all know
I'll be that blow
That tears you down
And buries your crown
The pain in my eyes
I cannot lie
The way I cry
Is built up inside
I cannot hide

The pain inside
I lift my fist
To hell with this shit
The pain in my eyes
I cannot lie
You all will drown
As I knock you down
You'll ask if I'm high
As I make you cry
You try and figure out
What my anger's about
The pain in my eyes
I cannot lie
Will take me down
As I terrorize the town
I need some help
To free myself
From the anger within
Who knows where it all begins
The pain in my eyes
I cannot lie
I need some love
To bring me above
The pain and strife
That has built my life
The pain in my eyes
Can no longer cry
I want my spirit
Yet I can't hear it
I want to smile
But its been awhile
I want to be free like a dove

I want to hug
Kiss and love
And show my love
I want to share
My heart's like beware
But I don't care
I need to repair
The damage inside
That makes my love hide
The pain in my eyes
Says a lot about me inside
But my heart begins
To heal again
I will change this fate
And build a love that is great.

THE END

And so we are here my friend.
This poetry book has come to an end.
Thank you for taking the time.
To read my poems and my rhymes.
I will keep it short and just thank you for your support.

Made in the USA
Columbia, SC
05 July 2024